# COSMIC CITIZEN

**KJ GoForth**

Gotham Books

30 N Gould St.

Ste. 20820, Sheridan, WY 82801

https://gothambooksinc.com/

Phone: 1 (307) 464-7800

Published by Gotham Books (August 14, 2022)

ISBN: 978-1-956349-81-8     H
ISBN: 978-1-956349-66-5     P
ISBN: 978-1-956349-67-2     E

# Acknowledgement

To anyone from my past who may have been hurt, my sincere apology. Know that each encounter every interaction led me to my Gift. Everyone and everything a huge thanks. Know that love flows back to those who give love without strings.

Flow with style flow with grace
Wear that smile upon your face

Become great become free
See the world how it's meant to be

Cast out doubt shed that fear
Stand in love see visions clear

One with all is in our grasp
It's our right it's our task

Leave your chaos far behind
You never know what you might find

Awake the sleeping awake in me
Be the one to set them free

Have we arrived is this our place
I see the look the look on your face

Long distance love growing restless in me
Show me your heart so we can be free

Alluring sent driving me wild
My turn to drive just for a while

Love affair so darn fine
Pop the cork let's celebrate with wine

Dance until dawn keep that fire burning
Vision of love all I've been urning

Lay down to rest embrace the next test
My heart is yours you are the best

Overwhelmed by excitement vision of bliss
Just one more time just one more kiss

I'll be here by your side
In you is where I hide
My love for you that has been given
Blessed to give you new beginning

Your gentle way your graceful walk
The one I chose to hear me talk
It's your fate a birthright not chance
It's your time your turn to dance

By your side always here
Never worry never fear
Your life is mine a true loved child
I'm your playmate go get wild

Dance on the wind play in the snow
Grow your hair long feel the flow
Wash in a brook carry my love
Step out and find heaven above

Majestic they stand across the land

Greeted with grace in this strange place

Doesn't seem real is how I feel

Tested and broke missing a spoke

Ready to fly life's truest high

Grinning because all of this love

Accepting it all because it's deserved

Leading the race slow is my pace

Determined to finish I eat my spinach

Meek standing strong nothing is wrong

Here to be great willing to wait

Back from the dead

Old skin has shed

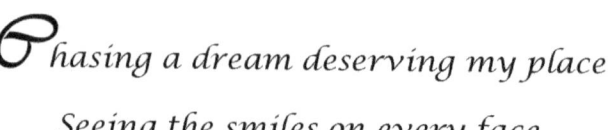

Chasing a dream deserving my place
Seeing the smiles on every face

Hard to explain what I've been through
But now I'm alive awake in my truth

Organized tools the ones that were hidden
Head on a swivel time to start given

Grateful for each breath exist in the now
Pure like the snow straight up I go

Detached from reality now back on Earth
Feeling the same love that I had at birth

Despite my transgressions a deture in life
All meant for learning, the hard way of course

Etched in my conscience alive in my heart
Time to start soaring and do my part

Wisdom in the tears the one's held back for years

Hidden in the soul the twin that was foretold

Gaining strength within the healing must begin

Shadows casting doubt makes me wanna shout

Realize the pain set free erase the stain

Shameless I exist crazy fucking twist

Freedom from above expressing only love

Manifesto of love after the fear
Write in my journals over a year

Uniting the planet without control
Love in the heart healing the soul

The past is the past it didn't work
Hearts have the answers wisdom does lurk

Peel that onion rid of its smell
Fear is a word it doesn't mean hell

The fear that exists is because of a book
Corrupted by criminals they are the crook

So open heart energy love the slight breeze
Ground in this place and sway like the trees

Cost of admission is only change
Don't let denial keep you in chains

*Back to the source back to the well*
*Universe crying headache from hell*

*Compressed like a spring squashed like an ant*
*Teardrops from heaven alive still to rant*

*Lonely but supported firm in my truth*
*Backward existing detective a sleuth*

*Brought up on the bottle not on the juice*
*Left to my vices now I know truth*

*Control is my enemy everywhere I look*
*Who's to take credit pages in book*

*Constantly controlling all in the now*
*Bitch slap the people paying why how*

*Shift is a coming open your eyes*
*No more living in fear or the lies*

*I got the number I got the trust*
*Wash over the earth down past her crust*

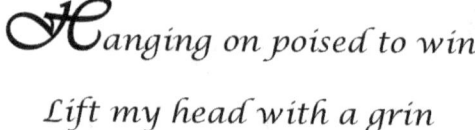

*Hanging on poised to win*
*Lift my head with a grin*

*Playing the game number one*
*Who knew it could be so fun*

*Execution on point liberate*
*Seen the future hard to wait*

*Breath in piece exhale pride*
*Grateful resting that I died*

*Distant memories boomerang*
*Blaring wisdom I attain*

*Hostage headed for a cliff*
*Break the pattern defeat the grift*

*Back to Earth for just a while*
*Long enough to laugh and smile*

Tested and hardened pulled from the fire
Love is the meaning true hearts desire

Understanding and wisdom free to the pure
Change the beginning drive away fear

Mentor of life trust in form
Carries the code as to why you were born

Details of past lives woven inside
The soul is eternal it never can die

It lifts us it guides us shining its light
Bringing us sunlight in the darkest of night

But wounded and corrupted it shivers in fear
It paints a cruel picture like trash in a river

The flow from the source poisoned by lies
Distracted insentient it doesn't know why

Detached and forgotten thrown out with trash
It's time for real change its needed at last

The weight of the trap heavy indeed
So much misfortune So many to feed

Weight of the World planted inside
Sensational vision in us resides

Conceptual Creation leaving the light
Come into existence willing to fight

Fight for what's right fight to be free
Suffer for the wisdom that's in you and me

The cost is our pain kept bottled inside
Confused by distractions control us they've tried

We are the solution inside us each truth
Find your light through the darkness earnest in proof

Tested and refined in your heart you'll find

Surrender to the pain mind blowing what we gain

*Truly humbled walk in piece*

*Brimming love no silence cease*

*Truly fortunate host of time*

*Tested daily love to rhyme*

*Truly poised standing tall*

*Watching waiting for the fall*

*Truly blessed vision wise*

*Future bright blinding eyes*

*Truly patient worries none*

*Childlike playful get you some*

*Truly companionate dig up truths*

*Never complacent stand for youths*

*Truly shifty stride for stride*

*Living learning stoic pride*

Fill me with sugar fill me with wine
Poison abundant dulling the shine

Bottled and boxed arriving each day
Unknowing humans sit home and pray

Distilled dilutions shadows and crimes
Choosing the numbness blind to the shine

Nightmares seem normal back to the drug
Which one this time don't want a hug

No one loves me I'm ugly and broke
These are the children for whom must be spoke

These lives are important to each their own
Stop drugging our children leave them alone

The cost on our youth taking its toll
Prescription writing corrupting the soul

Hearing the cadence the beat of her heart

Her breath gives us life to live on her harth

Joyfully wondering from here to there

Enjoying her wonder this truth I bare

A perfect creation forgotten no more

Least I give up pass out on the floor

Thankful for life I cling to her breasts

Enemy is coming I hide and take rest

Her grace ever presents a nature so pure

Lift up you head and imagine you're here

I hear her calling it's time to come home

Give up on society its headed for doom

Detached from the memories that kept me sick
I move like a butterfly as I pick

Perception altered mind free of junk
Overcoming deception humanities been punked

The light that's within us surrounded by dark
Patiently waits for just one spark

A spark of some truth as to why we are here
No distraction can stop me not even beer

This vail is layered it acts like a trick
When you first see your mind will trip

Magical and mystical better that drugs
It makes me want to give all you hugs

Eternally grateful for this life to live
I write these words it's what I must give

Forgotten are the many remembered are the few
Our gift to humanity lives within you

What is your gift don't hide no more
A conscious decision unlock the door

We are the forgotten slave to the lies
Beat down and walked on while evil lies

Rise up and remember why we are here
Fight back the evil without any fear

Love is our fate overcome hate
Evil's been winning since the beginning

The purest of heart will set you apart
The truth is in light trust endless delight

Concure perception live life as reflection
We have the cure to our hearts biggest fear

*A* walk through the past shiver and shake
Body aching hands a quake

Didn't understand the pain I held
A sickening bond strong like a weld

The ugly lies all pushed a side
Killing slowly negative vibe

Hard to fathom the spiral down
Lost and angry almost drown

Ripped in half by mischievous deeds
Empty soul dead end leads

Powerless no end in sight
Heartless helpless without fight

War was waging in the mind
Unsafe living completely blind

Crawling slowly to a grave
Hopelessly chained like a slave

Loneliness setting in
Think of your face and smile again
Those starlite eyes innocence pure
Heart entangled vision clear

I give you my love there is no fee
Together we can be happy and free
This time I wait clearing a path
Nothing can stop us not even math

The many nights I laid and cried
Worth ever tear life satisfied
How many times we missed this chance
The time is now for this dance

Embrace this love and hold on
The moon the stars the earth the sun
It will be ours in this life
A perfect union at last how nice

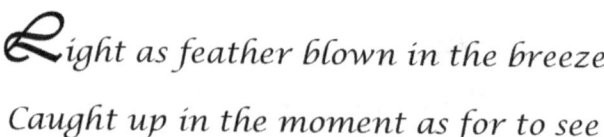

Light as feather blown in the breeze
Caught up in the moment as for to see

Heart is a flutter body all numb
Just one more second hold on don't succumb

Inspired by freedom creations true path
Look back on my life and have a good laugh

Memories are flooding the dam has been broke
This shit is real unlike the woke

Took time to listen that inner voice
My hands are still shaking no matter the choice

Love is the purpose I hear it inside
Write down these words so it cannot hide

The cup is so full it's over the rim
It fills up a pool so I can swim

This gift is amazing things are so clear
Hold tight to the wheel so I don't veer

*Out of isolation is birthed a vision*
*One where we exist without division*

*Why hold on to what is not working*
*Change what needs changing what's the frustration*

*So many times blah blah blah blah*
*We are the meaning we are the law*

*It is our power it is our grace*
*We are the ones who must run the race*

*Don't expect any change*
*Unless you're willing to face the pains*

*We are gracious we are great*
*We need love to resonate*

*Each so precious with a purpose*
*All creation late for breakfast*

*Time to rise up and let love glow*
*Eminating from our soul*

Needle to the head

Your hearts bleeding black not red


Dependent on the lies

Shifting sands don't compromise


Corrupted by the power

Souls stolen every hour


Glorified by faith

Lasting memories of hate


The innocent they die

While the war machine gets high


Insanity is quite clear

I will not live in fear

Strong here full of joy
Like a new toy

Life with direction
With heavenly protection

Free to be me
Wild visions I see

Enjoying the ride false pride set aside
Holding my truth awe inspired with proof

Love in my heart
Piece sets me apart

Not in a race
I set my own pace

The future is mine
Tingle down spine

*Late is our fate it's time I can't wait*

*Let truth be reveled for those who've be healed*

*Wait not for your death lungs without breath*

*Change from within don't let conformity win*

*Perceive with your heart it sets us apart*

*Look for the signs hold steady it's fine*

*Walk in the grace it's not a race*

*Appreciate life cast shadows on strife*

*Be thankful you're here even if it's not clear*

*Walk back the lies and trinity dies*

Protection and guidance in the light
Refuge found for the fight

Holly battle waged in war
Blood-stained robes nothing more

Power mad evil dressed like sheep
Wicked doers in a heap

Senseless killing all around
Blood-soaked streets soiled ground

Righteous noble for a cause
Not Gods laws take a pause

Blackness oozing from the veins
Fuel the fire life in chains

Confiscation of a land
Terror torture of the band

Widespread horror on this plate
Speak of glory nothing great

Please save me from these wicked lies
Hold me close each day I cry

At piece again white fire burns with in

Free to be me turned loose for a spree

I'm calling you out denial and doubt

Raised from the dead old patterns shed

Rejecting old lies they parolize

Accepting my fate I patiently wait

Hard to believe don't fight it relieve

Changed for good promise withstood

Living a dream purpose been seen

Holding on tight withstanding the light

Grounded in love fog lifting above

Cauterize the heart stitch up the soul
Bleeding profusely out of control
A fight for dominion no cost to high
Misled by a system foundations a lie

The toll is our freedom that we already had
Rely on yourself the governments bad
Corrupt politicians on either side
Lining their pockets with gold that they hide

The people are losing control taking hold
The commies are winning it's time to get bold
Weak leadership will strip us of God given rights
It's up to the people to stand up and fight

Stand for your freedom fly government the bird
The ones we elected they smell like a turd
Our system works and so it's been said
Keep evil from your doorstep its blood too is red

Sorrow and pain abandoned by love

Evil illusions hidden in drugs


Hopeless desires wicked results

Avalanche of emotions life without hope


Wasting away on the streets you call home

Cast out and spit on with nowhere to go


This human condition the problems within

There's a solution for healing to win

Conformity the killer get in line
Broken back bent knee define

Bullied controlled by the few
Don't let this happen to you

Stand up straight full of pride
Stoic heroes always survive

Lashings constant evil tongue
Danger eminent what's to come

Condescending bigots in our face
Disgusting shameless cowardly race

Creed of heathens blackened souls
Botched up righteous full of holes

Envy jealous greedy lies
Too much to bare it's time to rise

Hold fast steady in good time
Virtues patience time to shine

Ancestors with me slowing me down
Looking around me what has been found

Awe stricken dizzy spinning around
The earth is still sacred heart beating abounds

All things connected all things as one
Except for us humans we are quite dumb

Caught up in this moment right here and now
I take a long breather to contemplate how

Why separation what has been done
The souls of the many not having fun

Life is so precious life can be great
Cast off shadows let light hold your fate

A destiny a meeting only one truth
Patiently waiting for some kind of proof

Your video in life what will it show
Did you experience the soul's final goal

What is your purpose who are you now
Confused by the chaos the dark in the loud

If only a whisper could trigger the light
Humanity could be lifted souls set a flight

Pain and anguish that live in the mind and soul
Cripple this existence let it all go

There's always one spot in this video of life
That inflicts us with pain dimming the light

The grief and the guilt what does it serve
Conflicting the conscience dogma preserved

Why not face fear and see where it leads
This video will amaze shock startle and tease

Focused on the future the past has no grip

Higher self-healing there's no need to trip

Forged like and anchor holding me down

The Earth is my mother this I have found


The heart of all hearts created for the free

A playground for many especially me

Her Love is so real this is my truth

Beautiful and natural there is no roof


Peaceful I play in her arms everyday

Enjoying her grace that's here to stay

Helping her heal some of her wounds

Led by the light of the full moons


Captivated and conscience of all that there is

Gifted by presence much love to give

Respecting her laws as we are one

Basking in beauty having much fun

The hearts that are singing will become as one
Written down on the soul before time begun

Heartfelt liberated no longer lies
Reach out to the universe and get your surprise

Waiting and wanting for so damn long
Spiritually guided let love sing the song

Hardened by lies softened by love
Creation is real let your spark soar above

All from the same place there is no doubt
Open your eyes and let your spark out

If you only knew how special you are
You'd abandon society and drive real far

Creativity is our purpose stop living lies
The evidence is written on each person's eyes

Cannot sleep she's on my mind
Her beauty blinds me she's so fine

Soft light skin that radiates
Glowing eyes that penetrate

Heart so warm it permeates
In my arms could this be fate

As time goes by I realize
That sparkle in those starlite eyes

Her eyes that keep me mesmerized
Like bright stars in dark skies

I hold my breath to wait and see
If this love is meant for me

After a million lives or so
I think it's her my missing soul

Hiding behind the eyes the fear it never lies

Dead souls look away not knowing why they stay


Caught up in a trance looking for romance

Wasting all these years fleeing from the tears


Upended by the pain run over by a train

Barely holding on one more set back I'll be gone


What's this world about left my body now I shout

Sickness in my brain it's so heavy can't restrain


Can't take it anymore smash my face in to a door

Detached from my core am I dead or is there more

As the light fades away it's the end of today

Blessed by this moment free will and atonement

Spectacular horizon I give thanks for my rising

Glory to creation take pause for temptation

Existing by love set free for a cause

Not holding back no need to attack

Soul purpose giving it's time to start living

Past is the past it won't hold me back

Reaching this height I fly like a kite

*Caught up in this endless fight*
*Reaching out all despite*

*Past and present merge as one*
*Smile grinning this is fun*

*Hardly trying anymore*
*Body weightless like before*

*Wisdom flowing from my soul*
*As widespread terror takes its toll*

*Wanting nothing have so much*
*Gods true blessing I've been touched*

*Patient seeing the divine*
*Grapes all dangle from the vine*

*Tree of knowledge grows so strong*
*Bridge this gap and become*

*Seeing what's inside of me*
*A glowing light rest peacefully*

*One voice saying it's your time*
*Don't forget this you are mine*

Driving in the rain heart spills out with pain

The only thing that's clear is you're not sitting here

Fighting back the tears no strength now only fears

Looking off this ledge a mind that cannot pledge

Destroyed this can't go on fear laughing I'm its pawn

Chest pain growing worse love is like a curse

Shaken beaten down words empty disinvow

Sickened by the pain body aching where's my flame

Ripped right from my chest heart weak from no more rest

Please come take me now I am weary let me go

Not messing around straight to the source
Hitching my wagon to the only horse

Big in ambition creative in style
Full of rich laughter always a smile

Once drown in the ocean over my head
Now feeling free to write what I red

See the bottom is real no matter which path
To exist is to be born each time the past

Here to understand here to learn lessons
Here to experience life's trust blessings

Persistent in finding the pearl that we are
Rays of the sun brilliant a star

Detached from this reality come and I go
So much more to existing than we can know

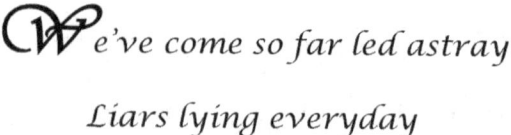

We've come so far led astray
Liars lying everyday

Without honor false pride prevails
Tedder toddler save the whales

Blacklist growing quell the rise
I can see it in the eyes

Envy breeding ignorance
Stripped of freedom no defense

Past transgression do expose
Worn out patters that must go

Trust in wrong place division clear
Corrupt leaders should have fear

Who's the people where's the power
Bent knee victims hose for shower

D.C. wicked political hell
Hope the corrupt soon find a cell

*C*alm your mind let it go

You are strong I'm telling you so


You're the one trusted by me

It's not your life it belongs to me


Know your safe know your free

Angelic wisdom how you see


Built to win throughout time

Bright glowing candle blinding shine


Your almost ready just hold on

Heaven's parting for the one


Strength in wisdom fills your heart

Magnetic lighting splits apart


Watch me give you your desires

I'm by your side put out the fires

Claiming the future in the now
Walk in piece gracious bow

Disciplined in honor harden by truth
Pulled from the fire after the youth

Watched and admired protection unknown
Frantic confusion set right from a thrown

Backward and upstream conformity denied
Own path to forgiveness destine to fly

Carving through hard rock day after day
Determined and committed for a long stay

This life worth living experience the gift
Fruit from the tree giving a lift

Brough back from the dead to live in the dream
Free from the shackles bath in a stream

Tested and challenged finish in sight
Comfort resting through the night

Beautiful visions could they be real
Dimensional travel breathless reveal

Burned in a memory past life it seems
No confrontation living the dream

Past and the present merge into one
Creating the future I know and done

Why in this lifetime why in this place
What cosmic force awaits our race

Distilled by truth child again
Worth the fight learned to grin

Support the love inner piece
Watched over always goodness grief

What's the purpose what's the meaning
Hold back nothing new beginning

Discourse causing rapid fall
Nasty comments on the wall

Coward hiding in plain sight
Like snake venom in the bite

Clouded judgement bent on greed
Control the mass's planted seed

Blinded vision no eyes to see
Narrow minded never free

Material holding status quo
Endless quarrel never know

Upright righteous blasting lies
Lacking wisdom big surprise

Condemning all that it fears
Hiding truth all those years

Grab on the tail of the dragon fly
Setting sights upon the sky

An energy so immense
Imagination the defense

Creation story's far and wide
Exposing flaws nowhere to hide

Tripped up begging to be free
Wisdom growing steadily

Hostile forces all around
In each city in each town

Sense of anguish brutalize
Wicked tongue dehumanize

Denial seething distorted truth
Dying helpless without proof

Ignorant victims paralyzed
Guilty pleasures tantalize

Societies story history
Nothing learned no one free

Reeling from the pain

Blame has struck again


Falling from my grace

The lies will not erase


Flowing from these tears

A lifetime plague with fears


Caught up in denial

Hidden by a smile


In this valley deep and dark

Blackened memories from the start


Crying out for all those years

Now I fear my end is near

*Is there a thing called piece*
*Where does it come from is it asleep*

*How many times must mankind be told*
*Piece comes to those who have healed the soul*

*Why live in frustration with all that angst*
*Society is dying it walks the plank*

*Hard to tell where it might end*
*Brain washed misguided no truth here my friend*

*Clearly seeing the cowards that lurk*
*Hardened by hate like some kind of jerk*

*The path to destruction it hasn't changed*
*Mankind rots inside who is the blame*

*Justify and blame won't matter in the end*
*Is your heart good why do we pretend*

*Denial is real it rips us apart*
*Bleeding out all that lives in the heart*

There's no disguise

No hiding those eyes

That piercing glair

The hollow stair


Confused and dazed

Thank white men's ways

Crippled by fear

Hearts that aren't pure


Riddled by faith

Caught up in the race

Dogma abounds

Discontentment astounds


Misery and pain

Blood flows on the plains

It's all one big lie

Soon misery will die

Waiting to see what shocker will be

Holding my breath for a while as I rest

Not knowing fate I sit and I wait

Holding back tears there are no more cures

After a while I crack a big smile

Seeing through haze this life I'm amazed

Watching for signs upright with straight spine

Hearing the sounds sweet music astounds

Experiencing this awe only one card to draw

It's time to get real and open that seal

It's time to get down who's wearing the crown

It's my turn to play so get out of the way

*Steadfast and steady walking in piece*
*Righting the wrongs slaying each beast*

*No safe harbor for resentment dogma or lies*
*Embroiled in a bottle one great disguise*

*Cloaked and shrouded all one big mess*
*Divided and concurred you know the rest*

*Whipped out and captured the darkness of greed*
*This seed of despair it shall not feed*

*Tears of the many the soulless command*
*You are the heethians this is our land*

*Misjustice at best this murderous truth*
*White men were quick to bury the proof*

*A cowardous people stealing for wealth*
*Fat and disgusting sickly in health*

*Why would I say it if it wasn't true*
*Negative energy is surrounding you*

*It's no secret you are kind*
*To get it all back you must find*

*An inner piece that lives in the light*
*Forgiving trespassers that trampled your life*

*Taker of goodness thieves in the night*
*Abusive bastards ready to fight*

*You deserve better you have a good soul*
*Free up your mind and let your gift grow*

*Emotional pain one thing to the next*
*Slow down a little and catch your breath*

*The truth is a miracle it sets us free*
*Imagine it's harmony and blissful glee*

Not here for pleas'n cuz of a reason

Say no to drugs say yes to hugs

Yes to love just wear a glove

Forget about hate before it's too late

Wear a big smile here comes the big trial

Be patient indeed stay clear of bad seed

Stay healthy inside fear will misguide

Walk in the light stay clear of the fight

Hold on to the truth you don't need no proof

Enjoy the ride this love will provide

Awe struck conceal truth will reveal

Through an open window blows

The sound of music to which I know

Caressing my body mind and soul

Lifting my spirit to a new plateau


With fear behind me conscience clear

Wisdom fills me no more beer

Hope for the future and all mankind

Someday soon all will shine


Piece with self and others here

From a place not quite clear

Honor dignity and good health

Pockets empty no material wealth


A drug user yes indeed

Humbled now I have no need

To return to that life there's no excuse

No reason good enough for that abuse

Where went the laughter where are the smiles

Mask wearing foolishness conformity defiles


What joy in that over reach real

Give me the facts not foolish speel


Where is the vision our direction our rights

If you don't like it here catch the next flight


Education is corrupted socialist ideals

Brought about by the rich so they can steel


Socialism is control you educated goon

I'd sue every college guilty of doom


Freedom is ours an inalieable right

The framers were smart they got it right

Responsible only for what I know

Humanity digging its own giant hole


Toiling at death consumption of greed

Feeling of envy children of need


To inspire the masses to find our true self

Put down your book find a good shelf


Free up your mind glow from the heart

Carry the goodness that sets us apart


The soul is amazing it won't let you down

So find it and let it spread joy through your town


Eager to know only my truth

Nothing will stop me I trust in the proof

*Steady I move through each of these doors*

*The doors that are here for us to explore*

*The treasure we find is ours it's been given*

*From the start we've been God like it's time to start living*

*I'll hold your hand as you start down this path*

*Imagine no fear erase all your past*

*Steadfast and sturdy upright on two legs*

*Joyful and happy no one will beg*

*At the end of the path the battle is won*

*Together forever living as one*

Conscience now of all that was

Weeping flowers start to buzz


Holding on to hope and love

Washing through me like a drug


Riding out this wave of truth

It's time to sing from every roof


Walk in grace and harmony

Waiting for my time to be


Watching waiting patiently

The path I walk has set me free


The higher self has brought me here

I write these word so mankind can clear


Away the past the hurt inside

The tears will pass if you try

Like a bird in a cage and a tiger outside
Clipping our wings so we never fly
We don't need them they need us
We are the prey dinner of lust

Fearful inside we shake and we hide
Drowning in guilt dying inside
Paralyzed to see
What we can be

Jealousy rains envy restrains
We are not living until we are given
Don't ask permission
Embrace the transition

Honesty inside
Will derail their ride
Nothings forever unless you are clever
Reach for the stars heal all those scars

*Victim from the start*
*Childhood torn apart*
*Reeling from the pain*
*Anger it's insane*

*Innocence been taken*
*Left on the streets forsaken*
*Self-worth in the gutter*
*Insides melt like butter*

*Abused out on the streets*
*Sex nightly on the sheets*
*Devastating blow*
*A daughter lost her soul*

*With no end in sight*
*She keeps fighting for her life*
*Holding back the tears*
*Boiling over with the fears*

*Stripped of all her pride*
*Only anger lives inside*
*Gotta see her through*
*If not for me then maybe you*

*I know you can hear me when I dream out loud*

*I know you can feel me like the breath from a cloud*

*I know you can watch me from that high perch*

*I know you can guide me so I don't do church*

*I know you can have laughter and tears of joy*

*I know you can see through dense fog on the bay*

*I know you can love me even though I am flawed*

*I know you can forgive me for disobeying the laws*

*I know you can write your name on my heart*

*I know you can encourage me to make fresh star*

Making love to the soul one word at a time
An insane expression a dance for mankind

Exposing a truth that's been locked up inside
Following intuition to where it does hide

No path is the same as to why we are here
Let love fill your heart and it will appear

Through kindness and love it's amazing at best
Twisting and turning there is not much rest

The strength and the courage to become as one
It's painful at first but now it is fun

Like a playmate who guides us and is always there
You're missing out if you're feeling despair

So follow your path listen to your heart
Don't hesitate it's your turn to start

Love is the giver to all that we are
Inside of our hearts we come from the stars

Here in this realm our soul seeks the truth
A path to walk forward there's plenty of proof

Reaching for new heights by being kind
Open your heart and see what you find

Compassion for one whom is all of our souls
Connected to the universe is what I am told

The angels are guiding those who seek truth
Enchanted they gather and sing from the roof

Love to all creatures love to all man
Give up on control let love fill the land

Love it's more powerful than anger and hate
Put down your guns and run don't be late

Love is our true bond to our higher self
It is our souls mission to live in good health

*Locked away like treasure*
*Seductive pleasure*

*Awaiting a playmate*
*Like going once first date*

*Emotions could fill the room*
*Vibrant like the moon*

*Heart smiling inside*
*Let's go for a ride*

*An unknown vail*
*Two realities set sail*

*Voyage to the unknown*
*Until it feels like home*

*Bath in its beauty*
*Rock solid shake your booty*

*Languish in the light*
*Even though its night*

*See it in the mirror*
*Lay doubt to your fear*

It was nice to have known you but this is the end
From the beginning I thought we were kin

Dividing this love that we have for a child
Your time will come there will be no smile

Good intention gone wrong they add up to nothing
Why can't you see through all the deception

What did you think would really go down
Dividing a love that was built from the ground

From the ground up it was all about faith
Believing one man could resonate

A love in his heart he knows it is true
But he will keep going cuz that's what we do

What is it you're waiting for
Did someone forget to lock the door

You creep around it freaks me out
It's paranoia there's no doubt

The things you say the things you do
The fear is heavy stuck like glue

What's in your past a fear so real
Out of control just stop and feel

Perception twisted by this fear
You should have another beer

Let paranoia control your day
Bend your mind like it's clay

There is no doubt you won't be free
This paranoia just can't be

This anger inside keeps coming back
I want to explode and mount an attack

I don't want to hurt you so give me some space
This anger will pass through like a race

I can't understand it I'll never know why
This control all around us makes me angry inside

What triggered it this time I'm not quite sure
It could have been something to do with the cure

I'm letting it out as my pen makes these words
I'd rather be happy than angry for sure

Already I'm felling my calmness come back
My mind tells me now no need to attack

This anger inside me is not my friend
I wish it would all go away

I'll hold onto love from heaven above and ask for this
anger to be washed away

Our insights been stolen and hidden away

A disaster is coming out of balance today


Our courage has been lost just waiting to die

Evil deeds on this planet shall soon coincide


Our wisdom's been lost the lies tell the truth

No one can think clearly else be labeled a kook


Our respect is nowhere just look around

This earth mother cries out you don't hear a sound


Our trust is placed somewhere somewhere that's not
clear

Disorder in the universe will soon disappear


Our conscience are rotten sickening the mind

I tell you I told you you'll get left behind


Our souls are like darkness emitting no light

Get ready to run you cowards won't fight

The problems we have are the things we must face
Their darkening our lives effecting our race

This lack of awareness from where we have come
Crippled our ability to become as one

The church's guidance is one thing I guess
But it's missing the point of eternal rest

The here and the now with the vehicle we've been given
Let go of your pain and really start living

Our distractions are many the pain feels so real
It's not why were here the truth will reveal

Society is sickened perpetrating with lies
I see it all around me it lies in the eyes

This higher self is worth the ride
I see it in everything it cannot hide

So imagine yourself living in peace
It's for us to experience after taming the beast

*A brave warrior once said to me*

*If you don't fight you can't be free*


*Any battle that will set you free*

*It's worth the fight you will see*


*How many ever arrows it will take*

*The enemy must die just like the snake*


*Your honor's at stake deep within*

*Pull back your bow let it begin*


*The fight's not over till your last breath*

*But don't worry it won't come to that*


*Stay true to yourself and you will shine*

*The outcome you deserve will be so fine*

Exploding from inside of me
These words I write to set me free

My past has haunted me so long
The pain is gone and somethings wrong

This empty soul no looking back
Am I crazy Am I going to crack

Nothing seems impossible
No one can tell me where to go

I left this earth and came back to find
The empty souls all left behind

The pain the sorrow spilling out
Impressed on me that there's no doubt

Somethings got to give you see
Cuz there's no love no harmony

So when you see me standing there
Looking with a distant stare

Know that what's inside of you
Is what I found and so can you

*From across the room I saw her there*

*When our eyes met we could only stare*


*Time stood still it seemed to me*

*For just that moment how could it be*


*My heartbeat raised my fingers numb*

*Could this be her my number one*


*This soulmate I've been looking for*

*She's the one I know for sure*


*We come together never breaking our stare*

*Our souls collide it's hard to bare*


*The search is over to my hearts delight*

*It's time for our love to take flight*

*A spark of brilliance in the sky*

*Lifts my spirit it's time to fly*

*A heart so pure it never lies*

*Unlock the truth and realize*

*For far too long we've been repressed*

*Open your heart and get dressed*

*Not knowing what may lie ahead*

*We seek the truth cuz it's been said*

*In every place around the planet every culture has a
story*

*All speak of tragic happenings all speak of real
glory*

*How much more trauma can we all take*

*What has to happen until a break*

*Let the floodgates open let it rain*

*Make sure this trauma was not in vain*

Once you find out who you are
No longer held back by human scar

Thoughts emotions they will change
Free from any human chains

Citizen of slavery we've become
History repeating cuz were numb

From the cradle to the grave
Doing what you told like a slave

Work for money get ahead
Beat down begging for some bread

There's a way become free
Written on the hearts of thee

Wash your conscience bleach it clean
Live in truth as meant to be

Conflicted by an emotion the one we call love

Willing and open to this beautiful dove


Her inner core lively and pure

Since of humor to be revived


Smiling eyes twinkle bright

Leave me breathless in the night


Hardly flinching always kind

Ever present in my mind


Welcomed distraction along this path

Breath of fresh air as we pass


If it's really meant to be

Time will tell and we shall see

All that there ever was all that ever could be

In our hearts our key to be free


The passion of experience begins

When old patterns disappear on winds


Hopeless despair and worried thought

Melt like butter in hot pots


Desperation dark and cold

Disappear no more hold


Beaten back standing strong

wisdom growing nothing wrong


Teased by greatness here and now

Accept the challenge with a bow

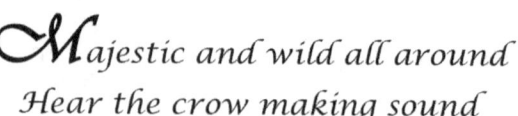

*Majestic and wild all around*
*Hear the crow making sound*

*A winter breeze passing through*
*Watch full eye for spring time bloom*

*She pushes back cold misery*
*On her heals the sun to please*

*Before she goes she brings the rain*
*Giving life to all her veins*

*Smell of rebirth in the air*
*Creatures rejoice everywhere*

*Cloaked in secrets to hide her truth*
*Poised to distinguish hidden fruit*

*Birthed from love the greatest deed*
*Here we languish poison weed*

*Back to basics reboot your life*
*Reach for greatness it's our right*

You are the sunshine in my day
Your laugh your smile your gentle way

Calm and soothing stimulate
Heal and healing verberates

Our cosmic crash burning bright
Keeps us warm all through the night

Forward facing bathe in truth
Universe beaming new found youth

A connection that can't be broke
Yours forever that's no joke

Lost in love tingling spine
Endless glowing will define

Sticks and stones can't touch me
Cuz this love is where I'm free

Never quite ready it's not too late
Lower the draw bridge go on that date

Passionate kiss quivering spine

Breathless and panting I'm going blind

Consumed by a love truest in form

Blast all the sirens and every horn

Tempted to give up everything else

Feeling the loss of the one's self

Electric and moving shaking the ground

Best gift ever is what's been found

Cherish and hold on nourish and grow

Love is the ending of the big show

Torture chamber here on earth
Giving rise to a new birth

Squeezed emotions toss and turn
There's many lessons to be learned

Frightening figures hollow shells
Primed for awakening gong the bells

Tattered lives torn apart
Isolation fearful heart

Destination in the past
This was never meant to last

Change is scary yes I know
But so worth it join the flow

The truth is in you just stand still
Clear your mind pay your own bill

# To Mom

Grace and beauty of an angel generosity of the saints
Giving to others without even a thanks

Living her life not a lie
Pureness of heart and twinkling eyes

Practicing kindness must surely pay
Look what she's lost and look what she's gained

Material possessions cannot compare to the
Love in ones heart despite the despair

Courage and composure give her strong will
The strength that is needed to climb that great hill

In a sea of empty souls you're a refreshing breath
Someone who truly loves life and lives it with respect

I'm glad we met this I know
You're happy smile livens up my soul

Until next time I leave you here my dear
Piece is at hand I know it's near

# In the Interest

Since I won't be making any public appearances or commenting on any social media platforms. Any person claiming this work of timeless inspiration is a fraud. When I feel the time is right. A face and birth name may be known. My hope is that this crazy aspect of my gift will usher in a movement that already has traction. Claim what's already yours.